LECTIO DIVINA

THE METHOD

JEAN KHOURY

LECTIO DIVINA : THE METHOD
AN AMORVINCIT BOOK

Translated from French
by Sr. Pascale-Dominique, O.P.

Revised by the Author.

Text and diagram Copyright © 2002 by Jean Khoury

The right of Jean Khoury to be identified as the author of this work, has been asserted in accordance with sections 77 and 78 of the Copyright Designs and Patents Act 1988.

All rights reserved. No part of this publication may be reproduced, stored in a retrieval system, or transmitted, in any form or by any mean, electronic, electrostatic, magnetic tape, mechanical, photocopying, recording or otherwise without the prior permission in writing of the publisher.

London

Preface

Lectio divina is an ancient Latin expression which means "spiritual reading of the Bible". It includes a wide scale of activities which can lead us from a mere reading of the Bible to a high contemplation and it is regarded as a treasure of the Christian faith.

This book focuses for the first time on a unique method on how to listen to God every day, through the daily readings of the Bible. It is a method which brings about a real change in our life and powerfully nourishes our personal relationship with Jesus.

Although many Christians read and meditate on the daily readings, only the classical way of "reading-meditating-contemplating" has ever been presented. This book revolutionises the method as it brings a greater clarity on the subject and proposes a simple and nonetheless efficient way to listen to God daily. It makes the action of God accessible to everyone and shows that our dialogue with God can be very real. So, from the image we may have of a "silent-distant-mysterious God", we are led to a new experience where he speaks to us every day, follows us and transforms our lives.

Even if this book was primarily written for a catholic audience, it can be read by any Christian who wants to listen to Jesus daily through the Bible, with the help of his Holy Spirit. Many churches propose two readings daily, and here we explain how to take advantage of this immense gift given to us by God in his Word.

London, February 2002   Jean Khoury

Contents

I

THE BASICS OF *LECTIO*

1. Introduction

The eternal and uncreated Word became human words to nourish us with his divine Life[1]. Like a beautiful stained-glass window, the words of the Bible let the Light of God shine through and illuminate us.

The Bible is like a sacrament; a visible sign of an invisible grace, it has a human aspect, the **words** and the **divine** life within it. The sacramental reality of the Bible tells us that through its words we are able:

1. *to receive God himself*
God is an uncreated being, which is beyond the grasp of our understanding. Through the human words of the Bible we are able to receive his divine life.

2. *to understand his words through our senses and intellect*
We use our senses, vision and hearing, to grasp the human cover of the words we read, and our intellect and will work together to gain the necessary understanding of a text.

3. *to be nourished by his words in our hearts*
The words of the Bible are carrying a divine life which nourishes primarily our heart or spirit. The words transcend our senses and intellect to reach this highest region of our being and transform it into God himself.

Without being aware of it, we may have a sterile attitude in the face of a text. The aim of the text is to transform us, however, we may remain at a level of reception

---

[1] "Through all the words of Sacred Scripture, God speaks only one single Word, his one Utterance in whom he expresses himself completely: 'You recall that one and the same Word of God extends throughout Scripture, that it is one and the same Utterance that resounds in the mouths of all the sacred writers, since he who was in the beginning God with God has no need of separate syllables, for he is not subject to time'" (CCC102). *Catechism of the Catholic Church*, edit. Geoffrey Chapman, 1999 (=CCC)

that seems to nurture our intellect but does not lead to true conversion. The Word then does not attain its goal because of our distorted approach, we are no longer receiving a Sacrament but looking at a text. And, considering only the text, we are no longer in touch with the uncreated incarnate Word, Jesus. Instead of listening, we stay on the level of a good explanation of the text or, even worse, that of simply projecting our own subjective feelings – i.e. our problems and desires – onto it. If Scripture is to nurture us, in both soul and spirit, we must be determined to let ourselves be disturbed, converted, jostled, and enlightened by what we read, instead of looking for what may comfort us.

There is a big difference between, on the one hand, "understanding" the Word of God and, on the other hand, "knowing" it. Understanding the Word leads to what Saint Paul said[2]: I know what I should do, but I do not do it; the Word is unable to incarnate itself in my acts and in my life.

Inversely, we can say we truly know the Word when, through an authentic and miraculous daily conversion, it really is incarnated in our lives. This is "miraculous" because it is an operation that touches the will and heals it. The will truly is ill in the sense that there exists a chasm between our intellect and our will, we know what we should do, but the will does not follow through. Saint Paul noted this when he said: I do not do what I think is right[3].

When approaching the Bible, two levels must be distinguished:

> 1 - the level of understanding
> 2 - the level of listening

In order to understand a text, one must make use of all the tools the intellect has to offer, for example diverse methods of exegesis. However, this is far from a true *lectio divina*, we need to listen to what the Lord says to us through the text. The first step leads us to understand the meaning(s) of the text. In the second step, its task is to be the instrument of the One who wants to speak to me today and nurture me. The text is destined to become a Sacrament. The Uncreated Word became flesh; it became a human word, not in the sense of being diminished or diluted, but in the sense that the Uncreated Word used the human word as a Sacrament to come to us and bond himself to us. We can analyse the material dimension of this sacrament (the literal, created human aspect of the text), but this will never give us God! It will give us an understanding of the text, a widening of the icon which constitutes its material dimension, but it will not give us the Uncreated Light. Both levels need to be maintained simultaneously. The aim is not to submit to what is irrational but "sacramentalise" what is rational, to make it transparent so that the Uncreated Light may come through. Although we can make an excellent and bright analysis of a

---

[2] Cf. Rom 7:18 and Gal 5:17.
[3] *Ibid.*

text, we are called to do something quite different. We have not yet gone into the process of simple *lectio*!

We can base all of *lectio* and its necessity on the words of the Lord: "apart from me you are not able to do anything" (Jn 15:5) and on the inner attitude of the Son of man described in Jn 5:19a-20: "Verily, verily, I say to you, The Son is not able to do anything of himself, if he does not **see** the Father doing it; for whatever He does, these things the Son also does in a like manner; for the Father loves the Son, and **shows** him all that he himself is doing". These words are said in reference to the Son of man, and consequently they refer to all men. We must "see the Father doing"; *lectio* allows this. The essential point is for us to introduce all our conscious activity into this movement, to slowly submit it to God's influence and to his action. This is the very basis of Christian life and of *lectio*. If we do not do this, we are simply self-constructing our own personal being, our activities, our daily programme, our Christianity, and doing so in vain[4]. We should meditate for a long time on the seriousness of Christ's words: "apart from me you are not able to do anything" (Jn 15:5). And, as a consequence: "I will show you my will each day and will give you what you need for putting it into practice". Anyone wanting to build Christian life or prayer life without these foundations is fooling himself, he is running away and straying.

2. Christ's central place in this process

a) Christ, the only mediator between God and man

When we are doing *lectio*, that is to say when we open ourselves to listen to God, we are facing Christ. Christ is the Word the Father has given to us, his only word, and he asks us to listen to himself attentively. Christ, who is both God and man, is the only mediator between God and us. We will see further on that the process of *lectio* is a process of incarnation. But it is the incarnation of the Word of God in us, the incarnation of Christ in us. We will never let Christ out of our sight: he is essential.

b) Christ reveals the Father

Christ is at the heart of the Gospel. In St. John he is presented with the specific function of revealing God the Father. "No one has ever seen God; the Son alone has made him known" (Jn 1:18). The Son allows us to hear the Father's voice, and to see his appearance *eidos* (Jn 5:37-38). By sounding the Scriptures, we are lead to the Son who is the Word of the Father and he gives us eternal life (cf. Jn 5:19-47).

---

[4] "If Yahweh does not build the house, the builders labour in vain" (Ps 127, 1).

c) Christ at the heart of spiritual life

This is the fundamental point of all spiritual life. Saint Teresa of Jesus asked herself for a long time whether, in perfect contemplation, one continued to consider Christ in his humanity, or whether it was better to be attentive to the vastness of God's divinity. The answer given by the theologians of her time was in conformity with the Gospel and Saint Paul: the fullness of the divinity lives in him, in bodily form (cf. Col 2:9) and we find hidden in him all the treasures of Wisdom and Knowledge (cf. Col 2:3)[5]. Saint John of the Cross, just like Saint Teresa of Jesus, invites us to contemplate the humanity of the Son with the eyes of the Father: "For, in giving us, as He did, His Son, which is His Word - and He has no other - He spoke to us all together, once and for all, in this single Word, and He has no occasion to speak further"[6]. To Him we must listen; and He is the one we encounter and listen to through *lectio*.

3. The primary impulse of *lectio*

The primary impulse of *lectio* is to introduce us into a relationship of divine friendship with the Lord, to allow him to speak to us and to (progressively) tell us all things: "No longer do I call you servants, for the servant does not know what his lord does. But I have called you **friends**, for everything that I heard from my Father, I have made known to you" (Jn 15:15). Telling everything to another person truly is a sign of love. "(…) the Father loves the Son, and shows to him all what he himself is doing" (Jn 5:20a). *lectio* is the eminent place where Christ-God will be able to speak to us, today, and tell us what he wants us to do. He will explain it to us: "and beginning from Moses, and from all the prophets, he explained to them in all the Scriptures the things about himself" (Lk 24:27).

It is impossible to assert that one should live by blind faith alone, opposing it to the understanding we get from the Word of God. Faith finds its sustenance in God's Word. If this Word is absent, faith becomes very meagre. Conversely, the Word of God, above all else, can fortify it. Faith is, firstly, the belief in a word that has been given. God speaks every day, he wants to speak to us: that is the basis of our faith. He will not say anything to us other than his Son, his Word, that he will give to us by little mouthfuls, in packages of light. We have a right, that of listening each day to the Lord who speaks to us and guides us. He wants his Word to remain in us; on this condition alone can we bear fruit that will remain for eternal life, "if you remain in me, and my words in you may remain, you may ask whatever you wish, and it shall be done to you. In this way my Father will be glorified, that you will bear much fruit, and you shall become my disciples" (Jn 15:7-8). We need to maintain a living and daily

---

[5] On this question, see Chapter 22 of the *Life*, the autobiography of Saint Teresa of Jesus, and chapter 7 of the 6th Mansions in *The Dwelling Places* or *The Interior Castle*.

[6] Saint John of the Cross, *Ascent of Mount Carmel*, II, 22, 3.

contact with the Word so that it may be active in our lives. People (and I am thinking particularly of those consecrated to God) who do not frequent the Word of God assiduously and on a daily basis let their faith and their dynamism die down, and easily slip away toward a human project and human thoughts. Their joy of living for God and of giving themselves to him, recedes before a lifestyle, which may be very active but where there is no place for God, it is without sap and without light. One's faith is directly proportional to one's contact with the Word of God. As the Psalm says: "Those who look to Yahweh, are radiant" (Ps 34:5). Looking to God means seeing His Face; now, His Face is His Son, the Son who speaks in the Scriptures[7]; His Face can only be seen securely in the Scriptures[8]. This is how the life of God shines forth. Listening to God implies becoming familiar with his way of thinking, getting used to thinking like him, seeing things as he does.

4. The immense importance of *lectio*

Lectio is extremely important for spiritual life. It brings us to realize the deep mystery of our vocation: the Incarnation of Christ in our Life, in our entire being. We are beings who have been given an intellect, a will and freedom. These faculties of the soul must be transformed into Christ; he must live there, but until that is realized, they are ill, and each one needs to be healed in its particular way. Through the contact *lectio* establishes between the supernatural and each of these conscious and active faculties, it opens the way to a genuine transformation of our being. Of course, it is inseparable from *mental prayer*, which works on the deeper levels of our being, but it is indispensable[9]. We feed our faculties every day with the daily events of our lives and we are not conscious of the fact that this food is often different, when not in opposition, to God's thought and will, *lectio* is the best activity leading to conversion. It accomplishes a daily miracle, the sole miracle Christ **wishes** to accomplish in us[10].

5. Basic activity of the Fathers, the eminent monastic practice

Is the practice of *lectio* something new? No, all the monks and all the Church Fathers practiced this way of meditating on the Word of God, and even today it is still an eminent practice of monks. However, it is not exclusively reserved to them; only, the monk is the one who, being a beacon and a light for the Church, gives the example of conversion and of the best way to achieve it. The Church Fathers were accustomed to the Scriptures, they all read, meditated and explained them.

---

[7] Saint Teresa of the Child Jesus said: "I open the Gospels to get to know the character of my Spouse".

[8] "The man who hears the Word (…) is like to a man viewing his natural face in a mirror" (Jm 1:23).

[9] In Part V of the main book on the *lectio* we will discuss the relationship between *lectio* and *mental prayer*.

[10] According to the Gospel, physical miracles are not necessary; but those touching the soul are. The Lord came to heal us and that is what he wishes to do for our soul as the days go by.

11

Thankfully due to the Scriptures they could contemplate God. The Catechism of the Catholic Church reminds us of this: "Seek in **reading** and you will find in **meditating**; knock in **mental prayer** and it will be opened to you by **contemplation**"[11] (CCC 2654). Furthermore, it may be noted that most of the Church Fathers started out as monks.

6. Listening, discovering God's will, its fulfilment

The aim of *lectio*, as we are presenting it here, is to listen to Christ, to receive a living and active word every day. This implies discerning the newness that is characteristic of a way of listening that leads to transformation. We can thus discover God's will each day. We are pushed to put this word into practice and, in this way, to sanctify ourselves, to really transform ourselves. What is intended is the Incarnation of the Word that God wants to speak to us today; this is like a little Annunciation[12].

7. The Readings of the Mass (a particular grace of Vatican II)

The Vatican II Council allowed the Church to realize anew the place of the Table of the Word of God in the celebration of Mass[13]. With the distribution of the Scripture throughout the liturgical years, the Church permitted God's People to be nourished more abundantly. Generally, the liturgy offers two readings, regardless of the Rites. In *lectio*, it is preferable to stay with these readings so as to eliminate our own human interference, as much as possible, from the listening process. The Church has already chosen the texts and so we receive them as coming from God – in the Rite of our choice. If we chose texts ourselves, we introduce a factor of preference that defiles the listening process. Opening the Bible "at random" is neither a satisfying nor a lasting solution. This is especially true because, when we do this, we are expecting to find an answer to a particular problem. Now, as we will see, we must not impose on the Lord the point he wants discuss with us today.

---

[11] This is a quotation from Guigo the Carthusian, *Scala* (Saint John of the Cross presents this same idea in Maxim 209 / Dichos 162). In his masterful work *Medieval exegesis: The four senses of Scripture* (4 volumes), H. de Lubac gives numerous indications concerning the meditation of Scripture and its meaning in Tradition. A good summary is to be found in: H. de Lubac, *Scripture in the Tradition*. One may also see the work on the exegesis of Origen, by the same author: *Histoire et Esprit: L'intelligence de l'Écriture d'après Origène* (Paris, 1950).

[12] We will discuss this in greater detail in Part III of the main book.

[13] This remark notably concerns the Roman Rite. "After a century-long exile, the Word of God has regained its central place in the life of the Catholic Church, this is an unquestionable fact. One could even call this a 'rediscovery' of the Word of God by the Catholic faithful, who for centuries had lost the knowledge of it and no long entered into direct contact with the Scriptures (…). Preceded and prepared by the liturgical, ecumenical and biblical movements, the Vatican II Council indeed (…) liberated the Word and put an end to the exile of the Holy Scriptures", E. Bianchi, "Le Caractère central de la Parole de Dieu", in the collective work: *La réception de Vatican II: 1965-1985* (Paris, 1985), pp. 157-185.

II

THE PROCESS OF *LECTIO*

1. Morning solitude

We need to begin the process of *lectio* in a quiet place of solitude. "But you, when you pray, go into your room, close your door, and pray to your Father who is there in secret" (Mt 6:6). The morning is the best time for this because the mind is freer and more vigorous, and the light received will be of use all throughout the day. "And very early, before the beginning of the day, having risen, he went out to a deserted place, and there he prayed" (Mk 1:35). Certain people read before they go to bed, and that is good, they consider that the Word works while they sleep (cf. Mk 4:26-29), and this is true. However, it is quite insufficient; when we want to meet someone we do not encounter that person in our sleep. Now, the Lord wishes to speak to us, he has something to say to our waking mind, and wants to enlighten and guide it throughout the day[14]. For these reasons it is good and even preferable to do

---

[14] The day will be like music, a musical variation on a single theme or even a single musical phrase, that of the light received. Other signs during the day will answer back to it, and the whole will be a concert played on the fundamental note of this light. God, like a pedagogue, continues with one and the same idea, but he develops several nuances. Therefore a day may often be consecrated to a single theme, one light beam. As the days go by, the light beams complete each other and, like in a puzzle, they slowly come together and reveal the entire mystery of God. In this teaching method, the angels play a major part, that Saint John of the Cross attributes to them – following the tradition going back at least to Dionysius the Areopagite – the motion (of the

lectio early in the morning. In any case, it would be useless to do it when one is tired. Our attention is important, because *lectio* is an exercise that requires pooling all of one's existential energy and, therefore, when tired, we are not in the best state for it. Doing it under these conditions would simply not be serious; it would be better to get rest.

2. Before Christ

So we are facing Christ and not just a text; and we want to listen to him. He wants to speak to us through the Readings of the Mass. We usually have two texts: an Epistle (or a passage of the Old Testament [in the Latin Rite]) and the Gospel. The references can be found on the liturgical Calendars. The aim is not to analyse the texts, nor to study them. Reading the Bible, studying, going to Bible-study classes, reading the commentaries of the Fathers, all of this is useful and does not conflict with *lectio*, but these things should be done at another time; as they are simply not the same activity as *lectio*. We may say to ourselves: "Now, I will listen to the Lord who wants to speak to me" but, if I have already meditated on the same text previously, the Lord will be able to tell me something "new" today. The process of *lectio* requires me to make an act of faith: "these two texts are God's words and, therefore, the Word of God". The same texts may say different things to different people and to the same, at a different moment in his spiritual journey. The Word of God accompanies the believer and gives him what he needs according to the spiritual state he is in. We must believe this. Let's take an example: A man taking part in an Ignatian retreat was to meditate on the texts. He already knew one of the texts as he had meditated on it before, so he left it aside. When the Priest accompanying him found out about this, he sent him back to his room to take up the "well-known" text again and listen to what the Lord had to say to him. He was truly surprised to discover that this text spoke "differently" that is, in a new way; but it is possible that the words now striking him were not the same ones he had noted the first time. Each time it is as if the Lord were marking a different word or phrase of the text with a highlighter!

---

morning): "There is no place for the motion of the appetite **stimulated by the angel** when this faculty (the will) is occupied by something else (i.e. other than God)" (Maxim 54 / Dichos 42) and also: "Observe that your guardian angel does not always incite the appetite to work, although he constantly **illumines the intellect**; therefore, do not wait to have a impulse to do virtuous acts, given that the intellect and understanding suffice" (Maxim 53 / Dichos 41).

3. Reading the two texts

a) The first request; re-reading

We begin by invoking the Holy Spirit[15]. A possible prayer would be: "Come, Holy Spirit, illuminate me, help me to understand the Word today"[16]. After invoking Him, we read through the text, it is normal to understand the contents of the text, but this effort to understand should not be transformed into exegetical research or deep study[17]. The notes at the bottom of the page may be used, but without being dwelt on. A clear decision as to endurance and patience is necessary as the body significantly slows down the operation of the intellect.

Let us then ask the Lord to tell us what He wants: "Speak, Lord, your servant is listening". This is the first request and the most important one because the entire evolution of the process of *lectio* depends on it.

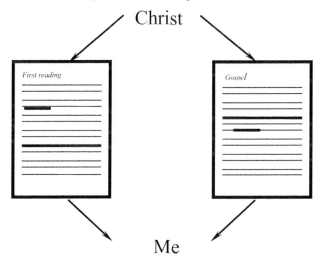

Christ

First reading   Gospel

Me

---

[15] "But since Sacred Scripture is inspired, there is another (the first is the intention of the sacred authors) and no less important **principle of correct interpretation**, without which Scripture would remain a dead letter. 'Sacred Scripture must be read and interpreted in the light of the same Spirit by whom it was written' (*Dei Verbum* 12, 3)" (CCC 111). We will discuss this question in part IV of the main book on the Holy Spirit.

[16] We certainly cannot listen to Christ, nor see him and understand his Word without the Holy Spirit. He connects us with Christ and **vivifies** the relationship.

[17] These approaches may be used at another time. They are not at all the same kind of activity.

b) The quality of the request; the example of the blind man

The quality of this request is decisive. It should be made with a pure intention, with all the energy of our being. The best illustration of the quality necessary for this first request is the call of this blind man[18] who had probably heard one of his beggar friends from another village talk about the Lord who had healed him. One day, while he is sitting on the roadside, he hears the commotion of a crowd. He asks what's happening, and someone tells him that Jesus of Nazareth, in Galilee, is going by. He remembers his friend who has been healed and now sees. His hope is roused, and he cries out: "Son of David, have mercy on me!" The crowd continues to pass, he cries out again, "Son of David, have mercy on me!" People push him away from the road; he is a nuisance. The disciples tell him to pipe down "keep quiet, he's got better things to do", but the blind man just keeps getting louder, because the Lord does not seem to be paying attention to him. Then the Lord turns around and asks him to be brought forward. "The blind man throws off his cloak and jumping up onto his feet runs toward Jesus". – What do you want? – I want to see. – Do you believe that I can heal you? – Yes. – May this happen on account of your faith. And immediately he was healed.

When this man asked the Lord to give him his sight back, he was not just passing time, amusing himself or asking out of intellectual curiosity. **His entire being was calling out to be healed**[19] and to see. He knew what he was expecting the Lord to do, he knew that he could heal him. We should have this same attitude; a request coming from our entire being, as if it was a matter of life or death, a desire to be healed, the desire to see, to see something more for today. And when we go to the doctor we are not ashamed of showing our wound, or wounds. In the same way, here we leave him free; we present him our entire being and ask him to act as he wills.

c) The first reading is not enough

After reading the text for a first time, we may retain a word or a sentence of the text that speaks to us more than the rest. It is therefore possible that the

---

[18] Mk 10:46-52 and Lk 18:35-43.

[19] As an illustration of **the question of desire**, we can read the following story:

"One day, the Lord was walking along the seashore when one of his disciples came up to him and said to him: 'Lord, how can we reach God?' The Lord took his interlocutor into the water and pushed him under. A second later he pulled him back out and, taking him by the arm, he asked him: 'What did you feel?' The disciple answered: 'I felt my life leaving me. My heart was beating so hard I thought it would burst. I frantically tried to breathe and to escape'. The Lord then said to him: 'You'll see the Father when your desire to see him will be as intense as your need to escape and breathe was just a moment ago." (Cf. *L'enseignement de Râmakrishna, Paroles groupées et annotées par Jean Herbert* [Paris, 1972], p. 300).

Lord is using this word or sentence to say something to us, but we are not entirely certain of this. The rest of the work aims at acquiring the certainty that this is truly what he wants of us. We usually have the tendency — the majority of the time – of projecting our own thoughts into the text. In fact, we come with our problems and impose them on the Lord, asking him to throw light on them and to give us a solution[20]. He knows very well what we need, he knows our problems, but often, he wants to deal with something else, with something simpler and more concrete. We, on the other hand only want to talk about what troubles us! We need to know how to let go and, from the very beginning of the *lectio*, entrust our problem(s). Actually by putting them on his shoulders, we are doing exactly what we need to in order to be able to listen. A psalm reminds us of this: "Unload your burden on Yahweh and he will sustain you (…)" (Ps 55:23); and the Lord himself says: "Come to me, all you who labour and are burdened, and I will give you rest" (Mt 11:28). He cares for all our worries.

In the parable of the sower, the third patch of ground is good soil but it is covered with thorns. Now, these thorns do not represent our problems, because always there are some, but rather they suggest worry, which like a rope or a heavy chain restrains our hearts. "[Other seeds] fell in among the thorns, and the thorns rose up and choked them" (Mt 13:7). "And that sown among the thorns, is the one who hears the word, and the **anxiety** of this age, and the **seduction** of the riches, choke the word, and it becomes unfruitful" (Mt 13:22).

Like a stone on the bottom of the sea, we are paralysed by worry, as if worry were able to change things. "And who of you, by worrying, is able to add one cubit to his life?" (Mt 6:27); "you are not able to make one hair white or black" (Mt 5:36). Now, these chains stifle the Word and prevent us from listening to what the Lord wants to say to us. We must therefore hand over to the Lord everything that preoccupies us. By freeing our heart in this way[21], we can consecrate ourselves to the "one thing that is needed"[22]: the quest for the Kingdom.

The Lord tells us: "Seek first the kingdom of God and other things will be given to you as well" (Mt 6:33). But, in fact, in the majority of our situations, we reverse the Lord's advice and we ask for "the other things" and, if there's a small place left, we put "the kingdom of God" at the end of our list. But this is precisely what the

---

[20] This way of imposing our problems, desires or requests on the Lord is comparable to a young lady who, sitting next to her prince charming in a secluded corner, puts her hand over his mouth and asks him to speak …

[21] This liberation is the result of an **act**. Nevertheless, the **feeling** coming from the problem may persist after the act, because it belongs to a more exterior sphere of our being.

[22] "Martha, Martha, you are anxious and disquieted about many things, but one thing is needed" (Lk 10:41-42).

Gentiles do, in the words of the Lord, as if a man's life depended on his immediate needs[23]. We forget that he is aware of all our needs and looks after them[24], and that we should not ask for perishable things. He does invite us insistently to "Ask and you shall receive" in fact, he tells us to ask for the Holy Spirit[25], the Will of God. In thus giving the first place to God, the heart purifies itself, since the purity of the heart consists in giving this first place to God in a genuine and concrete way.

It usually happens that, even after the first reading of the text, we do not find today's divine light. This may be so either because the text is difficult or because we lack concentration. It then needs to be re-read a second or third time or even more.

d) Not just ideas

The aim is not to pick ideas out of the text. Once someone asking himself if he had done his *lectio* well made a list of the ideas he had found, there were 12 in the first text and 5 in the second, so altogether 17: $12 + 5 = 17$. However, in reality we should come up with: $1 + 1 = 1$, since Christ speaks a single word to us through both texts[26]. We should avoid applying our intellect to the text, this would be a mistake. We need to be receptive, and that is the most difficult thing to do. Our intellect should not only be silenced but also "malleable" to the text, just like a light-sensitive film, while we wait for a word, a sentence to speak out to us, to imprint itself upon us and come to life, more luminous and more intense than the remainder of the text.

4. Rules of discernment: am I listening or not?

a) Two texts, one word (95 %)

Even after several readings of the first text, sometimes we may not find anything. (The order of reading is not absolute, and one can begin with the Gospel.) Then we go on to the second text, and read it attentively. In general, with the Gospel, things light up more easily.

---

[23] "Then he said to them: 'Be careful! Be on your guard against avarice, for even in abundance, a man's life is not secure" (Lk 12:15).

[24] "And if God so clothes the herb of the field, that is here today and tomorrow shall be cast into the furnace, **will he not do much more for you**, o men of little faith? Therefore do not be anxious, saying: What will we eat? or: What will we drink? or: What will we wear? – all things that the gentiles seek – for **your heavenly Father knows that you need of all these things**" (Mt 6:30-32).

[25] "If, then, you, who are evil, are able to give good gifts to your children, how much more shall the Father who is from heaven give the Holy Spirit to those who pray Him!" (Lk 11:13).

[26] On Sundays, in the Latin Rite, there are three texts in all (including the Gospel): $1 + 1 + 1 = 1$! It goes without saying that in the course of the week we may add the psalm to the two readings. Nevertheless there is one single light. The psalm may also be used to express our own personal prayer, but that is not properly directly our subject here.

However, it could also happen that we receive several beams of light and not just one. We do not know which one comes from the Lord. This brings out the interest of having two texts. Like two lines that can only cross one another at a single point, two texts can only touch on a single idea, "for me", today. One text filters the other, each text eliminates the elements that ought not remain in the other. On the following diagram the short lines on each long line represent the succession of ideas in each text.

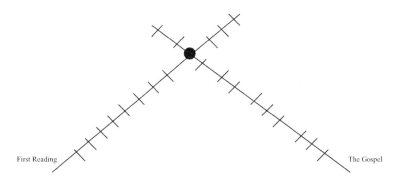

First Reading   The Gospel

At the end, after repeating and insisting, we notice that the Lord only says one thing at a time through the two texts. There is no need to search for words that are literally the same, for example "mercy" here and "merciful" there. Generally, the two texts are not connected, the first one may be an extract from one of Saint Paul's epistles, and the second from the Gospel of Saint Matthew[27]. Each author follows his own direction. The only common denominator of the two texts is that both are the Word of God and if we encounter the same idea in one and the other, this is either a mere coincidence, or we are starting to hear the Lord.

The fact that the Lord speaks to us through these two texts, with one single idea, brings our certainty to "95 %" [28], he actually has spoken and this does

---

[27] As days go by, each of the readings is continuous. In the Catholic Latin Rite, the first reading depends on the yearly course – even or odd – while the Gospel is the same. Conversely, on Sundays there are three readings (including the Gospel); all these readings are distributed over three years (A, B, and C).

[28] The number 95 is a way to indicate that we are coming close to absolute certainty.

not come from us or from our desires. This is **the main criterion** to be taken into account and verified. And, although we are going to give four other criteria, we should base ourselves primarily on this one because it guarantees the highest degree of certainty. Indeed, this criterion is itself the channel through which the light comes. It lets us mark out the light. Given its course (from God, through the texts, to one person) and given the fact that it is divine, this light is not multiple but "one". Until we have only one single idea, **one** light beam, we must continue beckoning God by asking for His Holy Spirit and the revelation of his will for us today.

In the following paragraphs we will discuss the four complementary signs that help us confirm the origin of the received light. Even if the explanation is longer, these four signs in terms of importance only constitute "5 %" of the weight! This must not be forgotten in the discernment process.

Let us now consider the four signs that allow us to complete this certainty that a given word actually does come from the Lord.

b) The four signs

The single word received has at least four characteristics. Before dealing with them, let us see what composes a human being. In the following diagram we see the two zones of our being: the intellect and the will.

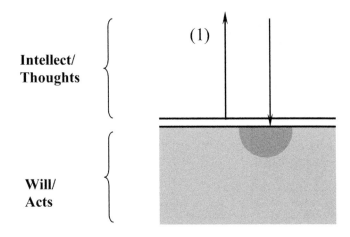

We will better understand what the intellect and the will are if we note the words of Saint Paul: "you do not do what you would like to do" (Gal 5:17)[29]. So, I have within me volition, i.e. the thought, the intellect, which recognizes the good thing to do, and then the agent of my activities, i.e. the will, the acts. Saint Paul remarks that, in him, and in each of us, there is a break between the intellect that knows what is good and the will that does not accomplish it. The diagram clearly shows this break. It is a gap in us separating the two faculties of the soul: the intellect and the will. We also note that the will is ill since it cannot accomplish what the intellect discerns. The weakness and illness of the will are shown by the grey covering the zone that indicates it. The number (1) on the diagram represents the call of the blind man who wants to see; while God's answer is symbolized by the arrow coming from above and barely touching the will at a concrete point, an area in our life which needs to be changed or of something to be done. In the diagram the area of the will in need of healing is darker than the rest of the zone of the will. This arrow pointing from above symbolizes the light received.

Let us now analyse the four most important characteristics of this arrow, which help corroborate our discernment.

i) A new taste

An example will help us to better grasp the characteristics and action of this light (symbolized by the descending arrow). 'The other day we had a dispute with someone and he was rude and spoke badly of us, or even did us harm and hurt us. Our heart is filled with bitterness. At best, we do not hate this person but we do not want to hear anything about him'. And just today, as if by chance (but, of course, there is no "by chance" with the Lord), during the process of *lectio*, the Lord gives us this word to hear: "Go reconcile yourself with that person, pray for him, bless him". This word is a new light beam that penetrates our intellect. It suggests a concrete action, and we understand that it comes from God and not from us. By penetrating us, this light received gives our intellect an impression of newness. This is confirmed by the fact that the indication God gives us is really the last thing we would have liked to hear today. Our usual inclination ("the old us") would have preferred something else, but the Lord highlights some aspect he wants to change in us, to transform within us. We feel the contrast between this new light and our usual light. This first characteristic, "the new taste", results from an "intrusion" of the Holy Spirit. Or, in other words, even if the comparison is

---

[29] Or in another passage: "The good I want to do, I never do; the evil which I do not want, that is what I do" (Rom 7·18).

too strong, it is like the apparition of the Lord to the Apostles locked in the upper room - He suddenly appears.

When *lectio* is practiced on a daily basis, a new desire arises in us, an expectation of the hour when we will meet the Lord and when something will be "revealed" to us. We can compare this spiritual desire with the human desire we have to listen to the latest news, to read the paper or when waiting for a letter from a dear friend or waiting to meet him. *Lectio* is really never boring. All these aspects together are the basis on which the first characteristic defines itself: the word has a taste of newness because it comes from God.

Scripture can be like a love letter from God to his own creature. In a similar sense, this is what pope Gregory the Great says to Theodorus, the physician of the Emperor:

"But, since he loves the more who presumes the more, I have some complaint against the most sweet disposition of my most glorious son the Lord Theodorus; namely that he has received from the Holy Trinity the gift of intelligence, the gift of wealth, the gift of mercy and charity, and yet is unceasingly bound up in secular causes, is occupied in continual processions, and neglects to read daily the words of his Redeemer. For what is sacred Scripture but a kind of epistle of Almighty God to His creature? And surely, if your Glory were resident in any other place, and were to receive letters from an earthly emperor, you would not loiter, you would not rest, you would not give sleep to your eyes, till you had learnt what the earthly emperor had written.

The Emperor of Heaven, the Lord of men and angels, has sent you his epistles for thy life's benefit; and yet, glorious son, you neglect to read these epistles ardently. Study then, I beseech you, and daily meditate on the words of thy Creator. Learn the heart of God in the words of God, that you may sigh more ardently for the things that are eternal, that your soul may be kindled with greater longings for heavenly joys. For a man will have greater rest here if he has now no rest outside of the love of his Maker. But, so that you may act thus, may Almighty God pour into you the Spirit the Comforter: may He fill your soul with His presence, and in filling it, compose It." (Letter IV, 31 (PL 77, 706AB))

ii) Practicality

The second characteristic is this, we notice that the given word is concrete, that it touches the ill part of our will. It is not some word addressed to our neighbours; we are not doing their meditation. Nor is it a theoretical meditation on some point of the Christian faith. No, this word concerns something concrete calling for a particular act or action from us, a real change of the will. The arrow illustrates this, its point touches our will, indeed it will be a particular area of our will where a change or transformation is necessary. We must therefore have a true desire for conversion, each time, so that the light may penetrate right down to our will. Otherwise, refusal and flight will prevent the light from descending and reaching the will. Not that it does not have this aim, but we impede it from achieving its goal. This shows us how essential the quality of our attitude is. The Lord unceasingly says to us: "I stand at the door, and I knock"; I won't force you, I don't impose myself on my friends' freedom! They have to decide to open the door. This is the fundamental know-how of prayer (whether of *lectio* or *mental prayer*, each according to its own methods). If one does not want to be healed, or even worse, if someone thinks that he does not need healing, it is useless for that person to approach Christ or his word.

So we see that this word, which Christ speaks to us, is concrete; it touches the will and incites us to a particular action. This action may be simultaneously inward and exterior, as in our example: "reconcile yourself with your neighbour". However, it may also be only an inward action which is necessary for example an act of detachment, of confidence or a sacrifice. No one sees it, but it may cost us great effort.

So the second characteristic of the light received in *lectio* is its concrete facet, which leads to true change, to conversion.

Scripture, a bitter-tasting book

"And the voice that I heard coming from heaven spoke to me again, saying, 'Go, take the little scroll that is open in the hand of the angel standing on the sea and on the land:' and I went to the angel, saying to him, 'Give me the little scroll;' and he replied to me, 'Take, and eat it up, and it shall make your stomach bitter, but in your mouth it shall be sweet as honey.' And I took the little scroll out of the hand of the angel, and did eat it up, and in my mouth it was sweet as honey, and when I had eaten it my stomach was made bitter." (Rev 10:8-10)

In fact, the word received does often have a bitter taste in our stomach; we feel troubled when this word penetrates and stirs us. When the light touches the darkness this provokes a certain kind of pain, a bitter taste. But this is transformed into sweetness and liberation. The bitter taste is actually a good sign; it indicates that the Lord has uncovered the illness and is working on it. If we want this light to consume the darkness, if we collaborate with the light, the darkness will be changed into light, liberation and new birth.

iii) A word that seems of "little" value

We might consider that the word He speaks to us is very "little". What does "little" mean? In our life, through the contemplation of the Cross, we came to understand that the Lord united himself to each of us in a unique way. Therefore, the Cross is not firstly an instrument for torture or a place of suffering; it is rather the place of our union with Christ, the clear and irrevocable promise of our union with Him. This union, the fruit he obtained for us by His death on the Cross, is called to slowly be accomplished, day after day. In fact, we are looking at the summit of Mount Thabor and wishing we were already there. The child within us wants everything immediately, and finds little indication in the Lord's words to him that would permit arriving there quickly. We are disappointed and we do not understand or, we could put it this way, the Lord wants us to be living fully, here and now, and we are disconcerted by his silence concerning the things that we believe to be important or essential and that, in reality, do not attract his attention. We do not see why the Lord gives so much attention to tiny little things. A married man might one day be asked to put his napkin on the table differently because, for the past twenty years, his has been placing it in a way that irritates his wife. And the Lord actually comes and asks him to do that! It is strange how such a little thing is given such great importance when there is a big project to be realised: one's union with God, or at a time when so many people are dying from hunger or AIDS. This is so because Christian life is made of little things and of faithfulness in little things: "Well done, good and faithful servant, you have been faithful over a few things, I will set you over many things" (Mt 25:21)[30]. Life on earth consists of this faithfulness in little

---

[30] And elsewhere: "Whoever can be trusted with very **little** can also be trusted with much" (Lk 16:10).

things whilst we, on the contrary, are looking at the top of the mountain. It is good to look on high, to dream and dream well, St. Teresa of Jesus recommends this. She asks her daughters to have elevated thoughts[31] and great desires[32]; but we need to keep our eyes on the little step in front of us, the step that contains within itself the entire mountain for today, for without it we could not reach the mountaintop[33]. That is the realism of the Gospel. What use is it really to think about tomorrow and to wait for tomorrow's directives, if we do not do today's work? "Each day has enough problems of its own" (Mt 6:34).

iv) Impossibility

Although this word appears trivial to us, it will seem impossible for us to put into practice. "I am incapable of going and reconciling myself with the person who hurt me because my heart is full of bitterness and paralysed. What should I do? I do know that this is the will of God, but I just cannot do it"

One day a young rich man came to see the Lord[34], at this point one might object that, as we are not rich therefore this Gospel passage does not apply to us. However if we look a little closer, we will find that we can be richer through our desires. Even if I am materially poor, I may wish to own a nice car or to have a good job. Therefore, I am still caught up in the possessions of my desires! It is impossible to fool the Lord, we are all rich. In that sense, this Gospel passage is addressed to all of us.

So it is a good thing to enter into the role of the young man by applying this text to ourselves and to ask, with him, for eternal life or, more simply, to follow the Lord and to be united to him. This is the goal of Christian life, and the love of the Lord on the Cross reveals it to us. He died in order to unite us with him. This union is not, as some think, reserved to monks and religious, or to so called "born saints". No, Christ died for everyone and for each one of us, for you in a special way; and you therefore have the vocation to be united to him. We must use all the possibilities he gives to us to receive all that he obtained for us on the Cross.

---

[31] "it will be a great help to us if we have sublime thoughts" (*Way of Perfection* 4, 1). "In other little notes I have written to you I have said this, and now I want to repeat it and implore you: always preserve courageous thoughts, for by doing this the Lord will give you grace so that your actions too will be thus" (*Conceptions of love of God*, 2, 17).

[32] "It is important to never let one's desires lessen ... indeed, if the saints had never decided to desire it they would never attained such high states" (The autobiography of St. Teresa of Jesus: *Life* 13, 2). "it is a great thing to have great desires" (*Conceptions of love of God*, 2, 17).

[33] This would be the asceticism of "littleness" in which St. Teresa of the Child Jesus was a specialist.

[34] Mt 19:16-22; Mk 10,17-22; Lk 18:18-23.

Here we are then with the young rich man who wants eternal life. The Lord asks him: "Have you observed the commandments?" And he replies that he has, since his childhood. The Lord looks at him and says to him: "You only lack one thing, go, sell all your possessions, give the price to the poor, and then come and follow me". The Gospel tells us: "The young man, having heard the word, went away sorrowful, for he had many possessions". This is the feeling we have when the Lord wants us to abandon something we are attached to, or to do something we are not used to doing. We are so deeply stuck in our habits that they have become a part of us, and when the Lord tugs at it, it is as if he were trying to tear off a part of ourselves. Then, "Jesus said to his disciples, 'Verily I say to you, it is difficult for a rich man to enter into the Kingdom of the heavens'" (Mt 19:23). And the Lord goes even further and insists: "again I say to you, it is easier for a camel to go through the eye of a needle, than for a rich man to enter into the Kingdom of God". In short, it is impossible.

When comparing Christianity and Islam (or Judaism), one would tend to say that the latter two are easy religions but that Christianity on the contrary, is difficult. But what does "difficult" really mean? The term implies that it is necessary to make an effort to put the Gospel into practice, and this is affirmed: "Strive to go in through the straight gate" (Lk 13:24), "for many are called, and few chosen" (Mt 22:14). So it is a question of effort. But there is a great danger in this, for one might be mislead into reducing life in Christ to a matter of volition. The Lord assuredly shows us in this passage that this is not the case. We do not accomplish our Christian vocation through the force of our will but rather through the humility of our imploration. We also encounter this impossibility of accomplishing the commandments of God, according to the light of the Gospel, in the Sermon on the Mount[35]. Here the Lord quotes the commandments God gave to Moses on Mount Sinai, with the introduction, "You heard that it was said", and then he put them under the light of the Gospel, "but I say to you". And, in this, we see that he wants us to fulfil the commandments deeply and radically; and, at this point, we realize that it is simply "too much", whoever gets angry against his brother shall be in danger of the Gehenna of the fire! And a man should not desire a woman in his heart because, in reality, according to God, he has already committed adultery with her in his heart! "Who can be saved"? The disciples let all of the Gospel's light enter into their hearts, it penetrated them from head to foot but they show that they are honest, "And his disciples having heard, were amazed exceedingly, saying, 'Who, then, is able to be saved?'" (Mt 19:25). In fact, someone might be able to leave everything, be detached from his parents,

---

[35] Mt 5:1-7.29; Lk 6:20-49.

even his children, his wife, but renouncing oneself is quite another matter! It is perhaps at the moment a person discovers his radical inability to follow Christ that he truly becomes a Christian for the first time! Saint Paul did assert, "Though the will to do what is good is in me, the strength to do it is not" (Rom 7:18).

Wishing is not doing. 'I wish to do the will of God but am incapable of accomplishing it'. We must therefore go beyond our inability. It is our normal condition, but on the other hand, it is necessary to transform it into a prayer, "Lord, since this is what you're asking of me and you want me to accomplish it, you can do so by giving me the necessary strength. Therefore, give me this strength, your Holy Spirit, so that the word you want me to put into practice may become incarnate in my life today". Saint Augustine says this in his own way: "Lord, help me to do what you command and command what you will". He asks for the strength of God (this is our second request) in order to be able to accomplish what God asks; and then he leaves the Lord free to ask whatever he wills.

When we feel difficulty in what God is asking of us, or when our will refuses to act, this indicates that the "old us" is still there – although we do understand why God is suggesting this action. Indeed, his request is in purposeful contradiction with our "old will", and the Lord wants to heal it. This repulsion and feelings of impossibility are consequently normal. He did say to Peter that his ways are disconcerting: "another will gird you, and take you where you do not want to go" (Jn 21:18)[36].

We clearly realize how and in what sense this word seems impossible to us and at this point it is important to remember that we need the assistance of God to enact the "impossible".

In the previous paragraphs, we analysed the first request and the light that comes out of it. We saw the main way to discern if the light perceived is really the light of God - as described previously in *4a) Two texts, one word*. We had also further clarification by verifying the light received through the four signs. Now we will sum up the whole process of the *lectio* including the second and final request.

5. The process of *lectio*; two requests

Lectio includes only two requests that bring two respective answers from God. The first request (1) (see diagram below) is: "Lord tell me what you want of me" or "let me see the step to achieve today". And the second (2) is:

---

[36] "What use is it to give something to God if he is asking you for something else? Consider what God is asking for and do it, for in doing so you will satisfy your heart more than with things for which you have an inclination" (St. John of the Cross, Maxim 93 / Dichos 77).

"Lord, give me your Holy Spirit **in order to** incarnate and **realize** what you are asking of me"[37].

The second request has the main goal to ask for the help of the Holy Spirit to realise what he asked us to do in his first answer. It is obvious that without his strength "impossibility" remains impossible. Following the second request the Lord replies giving us his strength to act; the received impulsion (and this is necessary) helps us fulfill what he has asked. He will heal our heart and give it the strength to pray for the person who has offended us, to go and pardon him. The response of grace is represented, in the diagram "b", by the arrow penetrating and transforming the will.

Lectio is in fact only accomplished when, in receiving his power, our will is transformed and becomes able to **realize** his light; the divine union of heaven and earth.

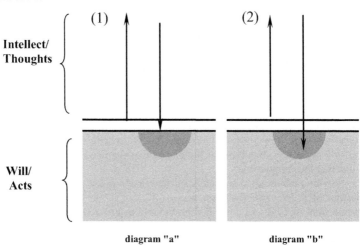

diagram "a"   diagram "b"

Attention should be paid to the fact that the second arrow goes beyond the gap separating the intellect from the will and touches the area or the point in question. Conversely, the first descending arrow, indicating the point the Lord wants to heal, does not yet touch the will. It shows and indicates but does not yet act. The Lord always has the extraordinary delicacy of never (or, at least almost never) pushing us[38].

---

[37] These two requests can be expressed differently, as Saint Augustine suggests: give me the grace to do what you ask of me and then ask whatever you will!

[38] A short remark concerning this, to illustrate the behaviour of God and the Saints: The Virgin Mary, full of grace, also had God's great delicacy and she said to Bernadette: "Would you be so

III

AROUND THE PROCESS OF *LECTIO*

The following paragraphs are meant to shed more light on the process of *lectio* and to help us to live and appreciate it more.

1. *Lectio* is completed through life; its benefits

As we know, the second request of the *lectio* is: "Lord give me your Holy Spirit in order to realise what you asked me". However the *lectio* does not end there! We need, with the help of the Holy Spirit, to put into practice the light we received. Only then the *lectio* is realized and accomplished. It is by going and reconciling ourselves with the person indicated by God that the "course" of his Word will have been completed[39], this Word ("go and reconcile yourself with your brother"), which came down from the highest heaven, spoken in the heart of the Trinity, touches the densest part of our being, our body (through the concrete act of reconciliation). This is the course of the word. It unites heaven and earth. It is always necessary to assure that the Word received, like a little light beam coming from the mouth

---

kind as to …".

[39] Cf. 2 Th 3:1 - "As to the rest, pray you, brethren, concerning us, that the word of the Lord may **run its course** and may be glorified, as also with you".

of God, truly is incarnated. Otherwise *lectio* will remain fruitless. Conversely, if the word is incarnated we notice remarkable progress and are certain to see changes rapidly occurring in our life:

- it is more ordered,
- greater clearness of the ideas and the acts accomplished all throughout the day
- a stronger faith
- a will that frees itself from slavery, and becomes more solid, firmer in the will of God
- consolation and strength coming from the daily encounter with the Living Christ and hearing him who speaks to us in our attentive silence and guides us in what to do
- and finally, staunch perseverance and resistance in life's trials.

In addition to this, it is good to note that one of the greatest advantages of *lectio* is simply the fact that our intellect is no longer at the mercy of the many thoughts jostling it, it has become disciplined, since it is nurtured by an intense light which illumines it from the morning on and all throughout the day. A man's thoughts are a major source of his suffering. *Lectio*, by reforming the intellect, educates it and protects it against worry provoked by thoughts because it transforms and replaces them through the light received. Instead of being haunted by worries, thoughts and the trouble they engender, our intellect is unified around the light received; this peace of mind is of great value.

> *"It (Scripture) enflames with the fire of love the man it fills spiritually. This is why it is written: Your Word is of fire (Ps 118:140). And this is why certain men on the way, having heard the words of God, exclaimed: "Was not our heart burning within us, while he was speaking to us on the way, opening up to us the Scriptures?"[40]*

2. "Lord, I have done, through your grace, what you asked me to do this morning"

At the end of the day, by revising our acts we can see if we have achieved what he, in the morning, asked us to do through the *lectio*. We will be able to

---

[40] St. Gregory the Great, *Super Cant.*, Prooemium 5 (PL 79, 475A).

say: "Lord, I have done, with your help, what you asked me to do this morning". It is a great satisfaction to find that we have been able, with the help of God, to achieve a "spiritual" step. Firmly accomplishing day after day what he asks us to do allows the Lord to hold the end of the wool ball (us), and so he may pull us in completely as the days go by. This will help us to keep our joys focused on the purest goals. Our happiness will be centred on fulfilling the will of God. In fact we won't try to look for any other joys, even if we have many imperfections and failures.

3. At the beginning we might find it hard to practice *lectio* for 55 minutes

People are usually surprised to learn that it is necessary to dedicate 55 minutes to this listening exercise and practice of the Word: "Why does it take so much time?", "we are not pure spirits!" It takes time for the light to pass through the spirit to the soul, i.e. from the most secret part where God communicates himself to us (the spirit or heart in the biblical sense), to the conscious and awakened part of our being (the soul: the active intellect and will). Because of it's weight, the body slows down this operation, it takes it time to perceive and to become conscious. Patience and perseverance are necessary. Moreover, the light received may appear a bit hazy at first, so one must repeat the request and insist until the word becomes clear and intelligible, until it makes sense to us, and this takes time. So why do we need to insist until the word becomes clear? Precisely because we have the right to an intelligible word, given that we are beings endowed with reason and need it in order to act. The one who gave us his blood, who died for us so that we might be saved, would he refuse us a daily word when he prescribed us to ask for it every day: "Give us today our daily bread"? He cannot refuse to give the word that can save us, a word indicating what is to be done each day. He asks us to apply our will in doing his will: "Thy will be done on earth as in heaven", how then could he deprive us of this knowledge, which is so important for our salvation?! He wants to treat us like friends and not like servants; and everything is said to a friend, nothing is hidden from him[41].

Subsequently one experiences this authentic and daily supernatural action, one experiences the strength and power of God's light, and this will lead to the desire to spend well beyond the fixed time, up to 75 minutes. At this point an indication needs to be given, since it is clear that one feels the need to stay longer. We need to know what is happening at that moment. We will have an

---

[41] "No more do I call you servants, because the servant does not know what his lord does, and you I have called friends, because all things that I heard from my Father, I have made known to you" (Jn 15:15).

attraction for remaining silent, and a tendency to adopt a calm, passive and silent form of prayer; we will put the Bible aside and wish to remain in the Presence of the Lord who is there. All of this is normal and it is *mental prayer[42]*. It is necessary to be conscious of the fact that we are then engaged in *mental prayer*. If we have planned to engage in *mental prayer* for a certain time after *lectio*, we should do this, and on a regular basis. If we have not, we should stop the *lectio* after a maximum of 75 minutes. Indeed, we should be careful that this "new form of prayer" does not become self-seeking, inspired by an egotistical desire to discuss the light we received.

When we read two texts, and find two passages that touch us, their content may seem general at first. It appears to be a general indication and advice concerning our life, but this is insufficient; we need something precise which touches our will and touches us today. The light comes through one or another word. Grasping the word, that is the first step; but this does not mean that the process of *lectio* is completed. We risk, at that moment, to interpret this non specific light by ourselves, either in a general way or by giving it the sense we would like it to have. We must go back and insist again. Of course, from this point on we insist only on two precise and materially limited parts of the texts. Our reading will therefore be restricted to these verses – given that they now have only a single meaning. We see the light become more precise and more intense; it is more incarnate in us and speaks to us today. It touches our will and consequently our freedom, calling for a particular action. The action the Lord asks of us may be for example an act of detachment, an act of confidence. Simply pondering over the same light, with insistence, allows the message it contains to become more precise, clearer, more distinct and defined. We should therefore never hesitate to insist on the same words received on a given day, this will only make them become more incisive and efficient. If we dwell only on general, vague and inefficient aspects... they will not give us life.

4. The required purity: the gift of oneself

The great effort of *lectio* is of humility, the effort of digging deep and of wanting to know the genuine truth about oneself. We must make this effort, and this is the price to be paid if the Lord is to be heard. We need to leave superficial thoughts behind and descend[43] into the depth of our conscience,

---

[42] *Mental prayer* (*oratio mentalis* in latin) is a deeper type of contemplative prayer that allows a direct contact between our heart (the summit of the soul or *mens* in latin) and God.

[43] "Jesus looked up and said to him, 'Zaccheus, quick, **come down**, for today I must stay in your house'; and, hurrying down, and he received him rejoicing" (Lk 19:5-6).

humble ourselves[44], lower our inner ear in order to listen to the Lord and not to ourselves[45]. This is pureness of heart and the Lord only reveals himself to those who are pure of heart. This is not a material purity but a pure attitude. Otherwise, if we had to wait until we are pure to meet the Lord, no one would ever encounter him. This is a pure attitude that we can control and determine; we are holding its controls and it depends on us. Of course, we can do nothing without God's grace[46], but the Lord always gives us the grace to listen in this pure way. And certainly we need to remember to ask for the Holy Spirit who will enable us, through his strength, to hear the Lord's voice.

Often we really only listen on a superficial level. On the one hand, we are prepared to listen only to what we want to hear and, on other hand, our listening capacity is determined by what we are ready to give to the Lord. And frequently one does not want to give anything at all. We give of our time, our money and what we are disposed to give of ourselves, but certain parts of our being are refused to the Lord. We forget that the Lord does not want our time nor our money, or rather he wants much more than just a little time or money; he wants our persons. And through *lectio* he wants to "transform us" (transforming our will in his), certainly little by little, but totally. It is really us he wants. "You did not ask for a burnt offering or sacrifice, but you gave me an open ear" (Ps 40:7+), as the psalm says. The Holy Spirit opens our ears so that we may understand that he does not want things of little value, but ourselves. Our freedom is the dearest thing in his eyes, and our giving it freely to him is precisely what he is waiting for us to do. He hopes that we will do this frequently and anew; this is his most burning desire. By giving ourselves to him each day we will come to hear his voice and let the Word work within us and through us. "You did not ask for a burnt offering or sacrifice, so I said: 'Here I am'". In these verses we see the difference between things given or offered ("burnt offering" and "sacrifice") and the gift of oneself ("Here I am"). In this way God's Word enters into us more deeply and *lectio* may take place. "In the scroll of the book it is prescribed that I do your will; my Lord, I have desired your law deeply in my heart" (Ps 40,8-9). The quality of listening, its "purity", is determined by the renewed fundamental attitude: the unconditional gift of oneself. This is what triggers the mechanism with God's Word permitting it to enter into us. The Lord tells us that our righteousness must abound above that of the scribes and Pharisees, otherwise we will not enter to the Kingdom (cf. Mt 5:20). For it to abound, the act of giving ourselves is necessary. We encounter the same

---

[44] "Whoever shall exalt himself shall be humbled" (Mt 23:12). This effort to descend unveils our heart and sharpens our capacity of listening so that the Word may act and lift us up.

[45] "Yes, the entrance to Scripture is low, and we need to stoop to go in" (Jean-Michel Poffet, *Les Chrétiens et la Bible* (Paris, 1998), p. 32.

[46] This is the "general help" St. Teresa of Jesus talks about in her *Life* 14, 6.

phenomenon with the young rich man (Mt 19:16-22), at the end of his dialogue with him, the Lord does not ask him for money or for time but rather for his person. Let us ask the Lord to help us to give ourselves to him so that we may listen and follow him day after day.

When beginning to listen in this manner we might encounter several ideas in our two texts; how should we then choose among them and know which one contains God's will for us? When the two texts converge to form a single light beam, this surely is helpful and quite decisive. But in order to acquire greater certainty in the choice of the words it is necessary especially for beginners, to proceed by self-renunciation, by abnegation, in search of God's will.

When, despite our efforts, we are faced with several light beams that touch us, we need to make a choice. The Word God wishes to address to us may be communicated by one of these light beams; or perhaps not. How then shall we listen to the Lord? If a light beam touches our heart and provokes our will, and not only the intellect and the world of ideas (which can remain very abstract), there is a good chance that this is the right one. Generally it is the one that costs us the most, the one leading us beyond ourselves; the one that "crucifies" and challenges us to walk a higher way, this is the one coming from God. We can more or less get our bearings by applying the advice of St. John of the Cross: "Strive always to prefer, not that which is easiest, but that which is most difficult"[47] or "for true spirituality seeks for God's sake that which is distasteful rather than that which is delectable, and inclines itself rather to suffering than to consolation, and desires to go without all blessings for God's sake rather than to possess them, and to endure aridities and afflictions rather than to enjoy sweet communications. Knowing that this is to follow Christ and to deny oneself, and that the other is perchance to seek oneself in God, which is quite contrary to love. For to seek oneself in God is to seek the favours and refreshments of God, but to seek God in oneself is not only to desire to be without both of these for God's sake, but to be disposed to choose, for Christ's sake, all that is most distasteful, whether in relation to God or to the world; and this is love of God!"[48]

5. Temptations to flight

Several temptations to flight present themselves and may become overwhelming at this moment, but we need to learn how to overcome them. *Lectio* is really the perfect ascetical exercise. Someone asked St. Anthony the

---

[47] *Ascent of Mount Carmel*, I, 13, 6. It would be good to read the entire chapter while not forgetting that its key of interpretation is the counsel: "First, let him have an habitual desire to imitate Christ in everything that he does, conforming himself to His life; upon which life he must meditate so that he may know how to imitate it, and to behave in all things as Christ would behave" (no. 3) and : "for the love of Jesus Christ" in the next paragraph.

[48] *Ascent of Mount Carmel*, II, 7, 5. This chapter 7 also merits to be read entirely.

Great: What is the most difficult aspect in monastic life? He replied, saying "Scripture" (in the sense of "bearing Scripture, suffering its weight of purifying and transforming light"). One must make an effort to remain seated. The Lord said the same to the monk Arseneus: "Stay seated, and don't move!" That is the effort; staying under the radiation of the Scriptures, of Christ speaking to us.

Here we find a list of the most common temptations:

- One temptation consists of only unveiling or exposing only a part of our being to Christ. This attitude obviously lacks purity.
- Another, more superficial one, is to want to do something else that could really be done at another moment. The idea of writing a letter or doing other business will appear to dissuade us from exposing ourselves to the light of Christ. And the demon and we, in our most obscure parts, are repugnant to this light. This therefore is the effort that needs to be made; support, and push forward to enter into the narrow path leading to liberation and true change.
- One might also say: "I know this text" and consequently be bored, *a priori*, even before reading it. Even though I assume I know the text I need to make an act of faith that this is the Word of God and that he speaks to me today in a new way.
- We might be tempted to read notes and commentaries. It is certainly necessary to understand the literal meaning of the text, but the study of the text and the reading of commentaries should be kept for another moment. This is necessary but with detachment from the present process. It nurtures faith in general but it is not the same as *lectio*[49].
- We can also be tempted to take a look at what follows or precedes our present text. It is necessary to be prudent when doing this. There is a risk of digressing from a legitimate search for information, permitting to understand the text and situate it, to squandering time and straying away from the goal of *lectio*. The boundary here is very thin and one must be aware, precisely

---

[49] It also occurs that *lectio* becomes concentrated on the savouring and the deepening of a term found in a daily reading. Throughout the process of *lectio* one evolves, learns, is formed, while gaining deeper knowledge and access to the Scriptures. One comes to have a new interest for the words, for their meaning in the Bible, in the Gospel, in the writing of a particular Evangelist or a particular passage. In this way we are doing exegesis, clearly at a simple level but this is helpful. *Lectio* then comes to be concerned with the discovery and the deepening of a term! The reflection seems to lead a bit away from the ideal of *lectio* and to take on an intellectual, exegetical character. But this is the point at which it is particularly important to listen attentively. For this is the key to *lectio*, which transmits us divine Life. The search for a deeper understanding of one or another particular expression is the way leading to the Life it contains. The two are not in contradiction to one another!

because the big peril in *lectio* is that it may turn into textual analysis. We receive light though in this way too, but it no longer has anything to do with a word the Living Christ may speak to us through his Spirit.

Indeed, the process of *lectio* consists neither in studying nor, analysing a text, it consists in listening and being receptive to the Word.

6. Insistence and perseverance purify the heart

One cannot insist enough on this kind of perseverance, this stubbornness in asking the Lord what he wants of us today. The first request will always remain the key to *lectio*, its seat, its difficulty and its battleground[50]. In fact, we should not talk about "the first request" but about "the *quality* of the first request". We need to be able to implore the Lord with insistence. One may even imagine that by insisting like children do to get a piece of chocolate cake, we plague the good Lord until finally, tired and bothered by the clamour, he deigns to condescend from the height of his glorious throne and give us a word[51]. God does not find this insistence, this stubbornness irritating, because it achieves something crucial: it purifies our hearts. This is so precisely because we are pushed in this way to collect all the dissipated energies of our heart, and to direct them towards God. Finally, our prayer comes from all the cells of our being, through the pores of our body that implore the mercy of the Lord just like the poor blind man on the roadside who begged the Lord to heal him, believing that he will answer his prayer. The action of insisting and imploring frees our hearts from everything that encumbers them. Our heart is like a lounge where all the seats are occupied when Christ enters. No one gets up to leave even though we invite him in! The people sitting there are our worries and attachments, the multitude of objects that encumber our heart and prevent it from welcoming the Lord.

---

[50] The process of *lectio* may feel like a battle, the hardest one; it is, in fact, the battle between the "new man" and the "old man" in us.

[51] This objection is considerable; St. John of the Cross presents it in *Ascent of Mount Carmel* book II, chapter 21. But this chapter talks about the **curiosity** certain people sometimes have when they try to discover something by a **supernatural means** and do not **listen to the word of God in order to discover his will**. And, of course, here he says that although God sometimes condescends to what is asked of him he is not pleased by this kind of behaviour. God's answering does not mean that this pleases him. He does indeed show – and we may be surprised by this – that God ends up by giving even if this is not what he desires. But St. John of the Cross condemns this kind of curiosity and even considers it to be a venial sin (in the same chapter, n°4).

We see this in the following diagram:

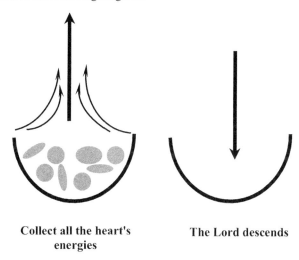

Collect all the heart's energies

The Lord descends

The recipient stands for the heart. The rocks in our heart are the attachments we have for so many things. And these things seem to have materialized in our hearts where they take up space, to which they have no right. In fact, the problems are situated outside of us, but the attachment we have for them allows them to live within us. On account of the idolatry of our hearts, the illusions coming from these problems – which are incapable of helping us move forward – grow into very solid objects, which reduce the space in our hearts for God since our hearts have come to bear resemblance to the creatures instead of keeping their resemblance with God.

"Martha, Martha, you are anxious and disquieted about many things" (Lk 10:41). Your heart is filled with a swarm of objects. But its Creator alone should occupy it. How is it that you place the Creator and creatures on the same level? Only one counts, and from there on we obtain everything else (in accordance with what is fitting and adapted to us, and at the right time).

The Virgin Mary was inhabited by God alone, because she desired nothing outside of Him. This is the basis of her purity; this makes her "poor in spirit". At this level, purity, humility and poverty in spirit are all equal. We are invited to imitate Mary's purity, precisely because God was seduced by this quality, "He looked on the lowliness of His maid-servant" he was pleased by her complete and unconditional availability to his will, "Let it happen to me according to what you have said". This is how she attracted God in her womb; and it is a kind of power she has over God. She gives us her heart, her purity so that we may imitate her. Through this whole-hearted request in *lectio* we purify our hearts. It goes without saying that when God sees our hearts pure and open, he comes straight in. As soon as he sees Mary's humility in our heart, he hurries, responds and doesn't let us wait[52].

Blessed are the pure of heart who, like Mary and with her, listen each day to the Word of the Lord and put it into practice! "Lord, may many people to experience this gift, to truly meet you by listening to your Word and living it; Lord, take flesh in us[53]. Amen."

7. What transformation occurs?

Through *lectio* the intellect is transformed. There is a passage from understanding to knowledge, as we said above. A part of the will becomes luminous[54]; Christ takes flesh there. This "piece" of the will becomes a part of the new man. In this sense, the intellect and the will unite, and the person progressively ceases to feel the gap separating, on the one hand, the thoughts and beliefs and, on the other, the acts (i.e. the complaining ill will). This gap slowly begins to be filled.

Let us note that the Greek word for "monk" is *monachos*, which means "one". Indeed, the ideal of the monk is to become one, to achieve the unification of his being, between the inside and the outside of the cup[55], between the intellect and the will, between one's thoughts and words and one's actions … We therefore easily understand that *lectio* is the monk's activity *par excellence.*

---

[52] Grignon de Montfort, speaking about the Holy Spirit, was to say: "the more he finds Mary, his dear and inseparable spouse, in a soul, and the more he becomes efficient and strong in producing Jesus Christ in this soul and this soul in Jesus Christ" (*True Devotion to Mary*, n° 20); and elsewhere: "When the Holy Spirit, her Spouse, has found her in a soul, he hurries there, he enters completely and abundantly communicates himself to that soul" (*ibid.*, n° 36).

[53] *Lectio* is like a small daily Annunciation. God gives us a word and he wants it to become flesh in us. Moreover, Mary kept all these things in her heart (cf. Lk 2:19.51). And this is what *lectio* is meant to accomplish: the keeping of the Word which is given to us each day.

[54] We are talking about a "part" and a "piece" of the will; this manner of speaking indicates that there are various steps in the transformation and that the will is not totally transformed through a single movement. But, in fact, more strictly speaking: "Since [the soul] has no parts, there are no upper or lower parts, nor does it have a part which may be said deeper than another, like bodies that have quantities; it is simple because it is not composed of several parts" (St. John of the Cross, *The living flame of love* I, 10).

[55] Cf. Mt 23:25-26: "Woe to you, Scribes and Pharisees, hypocrites! because you clean the outside of the cup and the plate, and within they are full of rapine and incontinence. Blind Pharisee! clean first the inside of the cup and the plate, so that the outside of them also may become pure". Certain Church Fathers also read the following verse in St. Paul in the sense of interior unification: "for he is our peace, who did make both one, and broke down the dividing wall" (Eph 2:14).

8. Keeping a written account

It is good to keep a written account of *lectio*. But we should not be in a hurry to write things down. That is not our aim. However, when two sentences or words are recognized as coming together, we may begin to write. These are the words we put to paper, precisely because they are the corner stone and the vivifying sap, the light of all that may be written. Next, we can prolong this thought to some extent, developing but without moving away from it, because otherwise we get caught up in human rambling; and the worst would be for us to believe that our own rambling words are inspired[56]! Writing aims at crystallizing thought, the light received, at giving it an intelligible form, helping the intellect and the body to realize what have been received. Writing also permits fixing thought. The written account becomes an objective witness, a mirror that lets us see ourselves more clearly. Later on, this will let us trace God's action, the thread of his grace and his direction. It is to be noted that, through our spiritual life, thanks to *lectio*, we move towards a progressive transformation of our being, it is conformed to Christ who is God; it is deified. God is simple (in his essence he is not composed, he is one)[57]. We are therefore constantly going toward a greater unity and simplicity. St. Augustine was to say that the Scriptures speak of only one thing from the beginning to the end: "Love" (and God is Love)[58]! For those who are not initiated St. Augustine's remark seems strange because apparently we find many things other than love in the Holy Scriptures, and especially in the Old Testament.

For most of us, writing and putting the light received down on paper will take some effort. This effort should not be evaded *a priori*. As we said above,

---

[56] Cf. for example St. John of the Cross in *Ascent of Mount Carmel* II, 29, 4-5: "I knew a person who, in experiencing these successive locutions, formed some very true and solid ones [...] also introduced others that were quite heretical. And I was very surprised [...] that any soul, after a few pennies worth of reflection and experiencing these locutions in its recollection, immediately baptizes all as coming from God and truly believes this [...] Moreover, the desire for such locutions and the attachment to them will lead these people to answer themselves and to think that God is answering and speaking to them. They get caught up in serious blunders if they do not practice great restraint and if their directors do not oblige them to abandon such discursive methods. For through these they usually derive more vanity of speech and impurity of soul than humility and mortification of the spirit – thinking all the while that something extraordinary has happened, that God has spoken to them. In reality little more than nothing has occurred, or nothing at all, or even less than nothing. For whatever does not engender humility and charity, mortification, saintly simplicity, silence and so on, of what value can it be?"

[57] The first thing we may say about God is that He is simple. St. Thomas Aquinas begins his treatise on God with this question (cf. *Summa* I^a q. 3).

[58] Only Charity emanates from all the divine pages: cf. *En. In Ps.* 140 and *De doctrina christiana* I, 39-40.

writing is in a certain way the first incarnation of the word that God speaks to us. Putting it down on paper gives it a form, defines it's outlines and thus helps us to become aware of this daily event, the living encounter, through *lectio* of our conscious intellect with the words of the Risen Christ.

Finally, writing is necessary, but it may also lead to dispersion, especially for certain people. It is an instrument that needs to be well used. The date and perhaps the liturgical circumstance[59] should be noted; they will serve as markers later on. The written account of *lectio*, of God's action in us, of the love letters he sends to us each day, form our spiritual history. However, "spiritual" does not mean airy, on the contrary, this dimension of our life is more real than its outer dimension. In fact, an inner world is founded and slowly begins to dominate (through its importance and priority) our outer life, which is often distressingly superficial.

9. *Lectio* is an authentic exercise of love

"One day someone asked St. John of the Cross how he enters into ecstasy, he answered that this was by relinquishing his own will and doing the will of God. Because ecstasy for a soul is nothing other than leaving itself behind and being raptured in God – and this is what the person who obeys him does, because he leaves himself behind as well as his own will and, having become lighter, he attaches himself to God (or 'sinks into God')[60]". This shows us that *lectio* truly is an exercise of love, since it supposes that we abandon ourselves each day in a loving, resolute and authentic quest for the Truth. *Lectio* awaits souls who love truth and are not afraid of it. It seeks generous and courageous souls, capable of questioning themselves every day before God, ready to be converted.

10. *Lectio* is a daily verification of this self-abandonment

Lectio is a great way for us to be assured that we are doing God's will. It is a way of verification, a test, a true and practical confirmation of our desire to love God; it tells us where we are in our love for God. Loving God is simply doing his will, and the quest for this will is at the heart of *lectio*.

---

[59] God gives himself through the rhythm of liturgical life, through the rhythm of the yearly celebrations of Christ's mysteries. It will be noted that grace is much stronger on important feasts and solemnities as well as during Lent, for example. *Lectio* will therefore be even more striking on these days.

[60] Maxim 210.

11. The consolation we receive in *lectio*

Because *lectio* opens the door for us to a true encounter with the Lord and to tangible daily conversion, it is also a source of great consolation. But this consolation is an inherent aspect of *lectio* itself; it is not added on, optional, nor is it a kind of gift the Lord bestows on those he considers weak. Saint Paul talks about "the endurance, and the consolation of the Scriptures" (Rom 15:4), God's action in us, his light, which illumines our intellect and the true transformation of our will, is the very source of all consolation. Searching for God's will and accomplishing it, through his grace, brings us the purest and most lasting joy and consolation. The Prophet Jeremiah celebrates this when he says: "When I discovered your words, and I devoured them, your words were a joy to me, and made my heart rejoice" (Jr 15:16).

12. The desire to convert oneself - the heart of *lectio*

Let us begin this new paragraph by some quotations from the Encyclical letter of pope John Paul II *Veritatis Splendor*. These texts indeed deal with the question of conscience and the borderline case of erroneous conscience[61]. This does not lead us away from our subject, since our everyday life, closely looked at, is like a case of an erroneous conscience, and precisely because each day we need to convert ourselves and be illumined by Christ. We are coming out of the darkness and moving towards the light.

"Conscience, as the ultimate concrete judgment, compromises its dignity when it is *culpably erroneous,* that is to say, 'when man shows little concern for seeking what is true and good, and conscience gradually becomes almost blind from being accustomed to sin'. Jesus alludes to the danger of the conscience being deformed when he warns: 'The eye is the lamp of the body. So if your eye is sound, your whole body will be full of light; but if your eye is not sound, your whole body will be full of darkness. If then the light in you is darkness, how great is the darkness!' (Mt 6:22-23)[62]".

"The words of Jesus just quoted also represent a call to *form our conscience,* to make it the object of a continuous conversion to what is true and to what is good. In the same vein, Saint Paul exhorts us not to be conformed to the mentality of this world, but to be transformed by the renewal of our mind (cf. Rom 12:2). It is the 'heart' converted to the Lord and to the love of what is

---

[61] In moral theology, the "erroneous conscience" is the state of a person whose conscience has been incorrectly or poorly formed. This person may think that something is morally good although, in fact, it is not. If this results from his personal negligence in the quest for truth, his conscience will be considered "culpably erroneous".

[62] *Splendor veritatis* n° 63.

good which is really the source of *true* judgments of conscience. Indeed, in order to 'prove what is the will of God, what is good and acceptable and perfect' (Rom 12:2), knowledge of God's law in general is certainly necessary, but it is not sufficient: what is essential is a sort of *'connaturality' between man and the true good*. Such a connaturality is rooted in and develops through the virtuous attitudes of the individual himself; prudence and the other cardinal virtues, and even before these the theological virtues of faith, hope and charity. This is the meaning of Jesus' saying: 'He who does what is true comes to the light' (Jn 3:21)[63]".

This is where we must introduce the action of the Scriptures as the Word of God which enlightens and illumines the conscience! God's Word is the sacrament *par excellence* of His light. However, " […] the less serious our conversion to God is, the less clear the Scriptures are to us[64]". This is why the person who accomplishes and searches for the Truth comes to the light (cf. Jn 3:21), and the Scriptures enlighten him. The first movement in conversion is to seek Truth.

Each person's first duty is to seek out the Truth and then to conform his life to it. In fact, sin is not only non-conformity of our life with what we recognize as the Truth, it is also and firstly the refusal to search for the Truth. There is thus a constant advancement in this discovery of Truth. It is the task that lasts an entire lifetime. The document of the Vatican II council on Religious freedom brings this to light: "all men are bound to seek the truth, especially in what concerns God and His Church, and to embrace the truth they come to know, and to hold fast to it[65]".

> "It is in accordance with their dignity as persons – that is, beings endowed with reason and free will and therefore privileged to bear personal responsibility – that all men should be at once impelled by nature and also bound by a moral obligation to seek the truth"
>
> (*Dignitatis Humanae n°2*)

---

[63] *Ibid.* n°. 64

[64] Origen, *Homelies on the book of Leviticus*, VI, 1.

[65] *Dignitatis Humanae*, n° 1.

"Further light is shed on the subject if one considers that the highest norm of human life is the divine law – eternal, objective and universal – whereby God orders, directs and governs the entire universe and all the ways of the human community by a plan conceived in wisdom and love. Man has been made by God to participate in this law, with the result that, under the gentle disposition of divine Providence, he can come to perceive ever more fully the truth that is unchanging. Wherefore every man has the duty, and therefore the right, to seek the truth in religious matters in order that he may with prudence form for himself right and true judgments of conscience, under use of all suitable means"

(Dignitatis Humanae n°3)

COURSE OF THE LIGHT	OUR DUTY IS TO	OUR FAILURE WOULD BE TO
from Christ → to the intellect	**1-** search for the Truth	**not search for the Truth**
From the intellect → to the will	**2-** conform our lives to the Truth	not conform our lives to the Truth

1- The light from **Christ**
↓ ↓ ↓

2- Our **intellect** must search for
the light from Christ
↓ ↓ ↓

3- Our **will** must accomplish,
with the Holy Spirit,
the new light that the intellect has received.

When it comes to the Truth, too often we think that we have already attained it. In fact, this quest should be unceasing since it implies entering progressively into Christ who is the Truth ("I am the Truth"), to receive a continuous revelation and illumination. *Lectio* is built up on this point: a progressive revelation. One may indeed practice *lectio*, but without a real desire for conversion it is useless. This is what Saint Teresa of the Child Jesus said about the quest for the Truth which supposes the desire to change: "I have never acted like Pilate who refused to listen to the truth. I have always said to the good Lord: 'My God, I will gladly listen to you; I implore you, answer me when I humbly say: What is truth? Let me see things as they are, so that nothing may blind me'[66]". "[...] Jesus, enlighten me; you know that I am searching for the truth ...[67]" Or elsewhere: "Yes, it seems to me that I have never searched for anything but the truth [...]" *(30 September 1897)* and again: "[...] I can only nourish my self with the truth[68]".

The words Christ speaks to the Pharisees, in the Gospel according to John, witness to this illumination that He came to bring to the world: "'I came into this world for judgment, that those not seeing may see, and those seeing may become blind'. And those of the Pharisees who were with him heard these things, and they said to him, 'Are we also blind?' Jesus said to them, 'If you were blind, you would not have sin, but since you say: We see, your sin remains'." (Jn 9:39+). Someone who believes that he sees does not need a physician. Christ can do nothing for this person, and he just continues on his way. But, whoever believes that Christ is the light and that he cannot make the smallest step alone, is helped forward by this very act of faith. He goes from knowledge (Christ has more light than I do), through an act of faith (plunging into Christ the physician and saviour) to an experience (that of being illuminated by Christ). "And faith, in its deepest essence, is the openness of the human heart to the gift, to God's self-communication in the Holy Spirit [the Spirit of Truth][69]". "Opening" one's heart, that is what *lectio* is all about; it is an act of faith.

Lectio is therefore a call to go, day after day, from subjective to the objective Truth. This is the passage from one degree of perception and progress in the truth to a greater truth. It implies that we leave behind our subjectivity while we advance toward the objective light. And this is the price to be paid for the realization of our daily conversion and of Christ's growth in us. "He who is

---

[66] *Yellow Notebook*, 21.7.4.

[67] *Manuscript B* 4.

[68] *Yellow Notebook*, 5.8.4.

[69] *Dominum et Vivificantem*, no. 51.

accomplishing the truth comes to the light, so that his works may be manifested as having been done in God" (Jn 3:21); "Every one who is of the truth, hears my voice" (Jn 18:37).

It is the word of Christ that illuminates us, and is the Sacrament of the light. We need to seek it out and remain in it: "If you remain in my word, you are truly my disciples, and you shall know the truth, and the truth shall make you free" (Jn 8:31). "He who is of God, listens to the words of God [...]. Verily, verily, I say to you, if any one keeps my word, he shall never see death" (Jn 8:44-51). The Holy Spirit is the one who does this by leading us beyond ourselves and permitting us to glimpse the light: "When He comes, the Spirit of Truth, He will guide you to the entire truth, for He will not speak from Himself, but He will say everything He will have heard [...]" (Jn 16:14). Through the Spirit and with the consent of Mary, the Truth is born in us[70].

"[...] the law was given through Moses, the grace and the truth came through Jesus Christ" (Jn 1:17).

13. Digging deep

"Every one who comes to me, and hears my words, and puts them into practice, I will show you to whom he resembles; he is like a man who, building a house, dug, and **dug deep**, and laid a foundation upon the rock. A flood came, the stream broke forth against that house, but could not shake it, for it had been founded upon the rock. And he who hears and does not act, is like to a man who built a house on soil, without a foundation. The stream broke forth, and it immediately fell, and that house became a great ruin" (Lk 6:47-49). "Listening to the words of Christ" and "putting them into practice", that is **"digging deep"** and "laying foundations". The more we do *lectio*, the more we dig deep, going down into ourselves and allowing God to descend within us. In fact, we are the one's who let God descend – or not – into our depths. This depends on the quality of our listening. Digging deep, means descending into ourselves, letting the light penetrate our dark regions, at our deepest roots and our shadows. This depends on whether we open our door to Him or not; our freedom decides this. Our will to descend and to dig deeply within ourselves, this costs us a lot, yet it depends on us and solely on us. Facing the light, letting ourselves be illuminated by the light from the Word of God, that is our own task. We must face the Word, confront it, swallow it and digest it. This requires that we love the Truth, with a resolute attitude and a virile spirituality, and the desire that the light may vanquish our shadows.

God's action in us does not take place on the surface. It is orientated toward the depths. This action infiltrates our inner tissue and frees it, making it subtle and

---

[70] This point will be explained in the book "Lectio Divina II, Mary and the Spirit", Mary and *lectio*.

deifying it. This is why deep silent prayer, *mental prayer,* is founded on *lectio*; precisely because *lectio* opens up the way for God so that he may go ever deeper in us through *mental prayer.* The effort of *lectio* opens the door to the divine Beam of contemplation during *mental prayer.* In an ordinary way, without this effort God does not permit himself to enter into us through his supernatural action (the "special help" of Teresa of Jesus)[71].

14- Vade mecum

We can now give a short description of the steps to follow in the practice of *lectio.* There are 7 steps in all:

1- Sit down

in a quiet and solitary place - in the morning if possible.

2- Ask

the Holy Spirit for help in listening to the Lord.

3- Re-read

the two texts until they reveal one single and *clear light* for today.

4- Ask

for the strength of the Holy Spirit in order to put the *light* received into practice.

5- Write

down briefly the *light* received.

6- Put into practice

the *word* received today.

7- Verify

at the end of the day that we have incarnated the *word,*
and give thanks to God for it.

---

[71] We discuss these questions in the book *Lectio III, Lectio and Daily Life,* part V.

Conclusion

This method brings a real excitement and a deep joy into daily life. Every morning we can look forward to something new that Jesus will tell us. We are no longer "lonely" because the Guide is here and he is truly accessible. The channel to reach him is now in our hands. Many people have discovered this way to have a daily and living contact with Jesus, a connection that really changes their lives and brings God's Light into it.

The third petition of the Our Father says: "Thy will be done on earth as it is in heaven". Through the *Lectio,* having first access to the knowledge of the will of God (which is to "see" Him at work like the Son does), we may then accomplish His will. "The Son is not able to **do** anything of himself, if he may not **see** the Father doing it; for whatever things He may do, these also the Son does in a like manner; for the Father loves the Son, and shows to him all things that He himself does" (Jn 5:19-20).

We may conclude with this prayer which sums up the centre of *lectio divina.*

"Answer the prayer of your People,
Lord, in your kindness:
*give to each person the clear vision
of what he must do
and the strength to do it.*"[72] Amen.

---

[72] *Collect* of the first week of Ordinary Time in the liturgy of the Latin rite.

Printed in Great Britain
by Amazon

40785752R00030